REJECTED
but
NOT DEJECTED

Nadine Blackwood-Barnes

ISBN 978-1-64458-503-0 (paperback)
ISBN 978-1-64458-504-7 (digital)

Christian Faith Publishing, Inc.
832 Park Avenue
Meadville, PA 16335
www.christianfaithpublishing.com

Printed in the United States of America

First and foremost, to my mother Desrene Blackwood. I thank her for bringing me into this world. You are a great mother who loves and takes care of your family with love. You also set the stage of keeping a Christian home. Secondly, to my church mother, Paulette Shuballie, you took me under your wings at the age of seventeen and stood with me as I chase passionately after God. Thirdly, to my late First Lady, Michele Harding. I will never forget the quiet powerful woman that you are and for the eighteen years we worshiped together. You remained faithful all the way to the end. I will never forget you… the last thing that you did for me was to sow a hundred dollar seed for me before you passed. While you were dying, you sowed a seed that I, Pastor Nadine Blackwood-Barnes will live. I will always carry you in my heart. Finally, to all women from all walks of life: rejection won't kill you. You can survive it. Don't let despair set in; it will destroy you. Lift up your heads and know that you are a survivor. You shall live and not die, to declare the works of almighty God. Amen!

INTRODUCTION

Rejection is one word that I believe we can all agree that we wish didn't exit. It has to do with us coming to grips that at some point in our lives we will experience rejection. Rejection is defined in the dictionary as "inadequate, to refuse to have, take or recognize." There are various forms of rejection, whether it is personal, social or any other kind. Rejection does affect your self-esteem. In life, no one wants to find themselves in this place. As a child, when games are being played and it comes to choosing sides, no one wants to be the last to be chosen. But at times, you end up being chosen last. This makes you feel as though you are the worst one. Yet as a young and naive kid in that moment being rejected is the worst thing ever. To be quite honest, it leaves a gloom over the day. It even takes over and shows up on your face. Rejection can be compared to a plague that you don't want to ever happen to you. Yet in life at one time or another, we will end up experiencing some form of rejection.

As an adult, we face rejection in many different levels. We may be rejected by family, jobs, friends, loved ones, and spouse. It doesn't matter the source of the rejection; the pain of it hits you like a ton of bricks. However, it is how we deal with the rejection that determines the outcome of our mind-set and how we will move our lives along. Also, our actions and reactions will play a vital part as we journey through life.

In this book, I will talk from my personal experience of rejection. How I dealt with it. How the Holy Spirit carried me through this valley. Also, how the Spirit of the Lord gave me words of comfort and birthed a ministry to hurting women in me. Come, let us take this journey together.

CHAPTER 1

The Early Years

I have always been a very shy child, and as I matured into a young lady, it stayed that way. I matured into an adult, and rejection was something I didn't want to deal with. I thought if I avoided certain things or if I didn't date, then my heart would be protected. So basically, I was very much a loner. The older I got, the harder it was to break out of my shell. I migrated to the United States as a young teenager. I spent most of my time trying to adopt to a new system, so boyfriend was nowhere on the agenda. I also grew up in a Christian home, so I was always aware of the Lord. I went to church with my family, and I was drawn to the Lord. I love the Lord with all my heart, soul, and might. I had guys who liked me, and I liked as well; but I always take the high road, and as I put it long ago, "the road runner" had nothing on me. I had a schoolmate back home who I cared about deeply; but I lived here, and he lived in Jamaica, so it wasn't going to work. Fast-Forward to the age of my late twenties, I called him and asked him if he was going to give his heart to the Lord, and he said, "I love God," but he wasn't ready. It was during this conversation I told him goodbye; I chose Jesus over him. It was painful, but I just lived my life from then on all for Jesus.

I wasn't looking for anyone. I loved my life serving the Lord and being there for my family. I had a church mother who helped me with my walk with God. She worried for me because I cling to older, more mature persons, and I barely had friends of the same age group. It was all about God for me. I first saw him at the church where I worship. He wasn't a member; he was the church musician. I didn't know much about him other than that. The only time we had interaction was on a ministry level. I was on the praise-and-worship team, and I was also one of the moderator of the worship services. After a while, he approached me. It was to ask me to help him and his dad with a concert that they were putting together. This was how I found out that his dad is a bishop. I helped with the concert and then went about my life as usual. We never had anything going on otherwise. As time progressed, I came to realize that he had a daughter and that he was married. It was hi, hello, and God bless you. I didn't know anything more than the obvious, and I never inquired about him. My mind was totally fixed on God. There was a brother in the church who showed some interest, and it was my church mother who said to me, "Nadine, if you don't talk to anyone, how would you know who God has for you." That never worked out, and the Lord knew best. It was the year 2005 when he reached out to me again. This was also the year God revealed to me my calling to ministry, so I was totally focusing on my studies. He would call once in a while, but the conversations were usually short. I would encourage him to stay close to God. There was absolutely no dating. As time progressed, he expressed his interest in me. I asked him what about his family? It was then he told me that he has been sharing apartment with his best friend for over a year now. He said that he was separated, and they both have moved on. I still remained reserved and just be his friend. He was in a difficult spot because he wasn't legal in the country. I would pray for him, and God opened doors miraculously where he could work and help himself. I told him point blank that I am a homebody, and I don't go anywhere; and most of all, if he hasn't finalized the separation then don't look this direction because I fear God.

To be quite honest, no matter how much time he tried, I had so many red tapes and wall up that he couldn't get through. Finally, one day in 2006, he asked me to go to the movies with him. I told him no as usual, but then after much persuasion, I told him I would only go to a matinee. This was the only time I ever went out with him. He got divorced, and he kept in touch. As time goes on he expressed his interest for a relationship, and that was when we would talk on the phone. I still lived at my parent's house where I gave them a small change for the room I was living in. I still didn't go on any romantic dates with him, but I have gone to a few church concerts and visited his father's church. He came by my parents' house if he's in the neighborhood, but not too often and not to spend the night. I am very strict, and my parents even though I was a grown woman was even stricter. He would sit and talk to me and watched me while I cook. I had a car, and he lived in the same borough as I did, so sometimes he would ask me for a ride, and I would drop him home. I wasn't the only one enforcing the straight walk. My father, mother, and siblings bear witness to what I'm saying. He was afraid of my dad. We continued to talk, and eventually, the marriage word came up. We discussed it, but most importantly, I prayed to God about it. I asked my best friend, my church mother who knew me from I was seventeen and others to pray as well.

The Holy Spirit gave me the okay to marry him. He gave me words of comfort and signs to let me know he has given me his blessings. I still didn't rush into it. I said to the Holy Spirit, "You are giving me the okay, but why do I sensed that he comes with a lot of trouble." I waited on those whom I had asked to pray, and they all said the Lord is with us. Therefore, I went about preparing for the wedding. The date was set for September 8, 2007. It was a beautiful day as the Lord had promised. The atmosphere even in the church was saturated with the presence and the anointing of God. A few people as the spirit swept over worshiped and spoke in other tongues. Along the way, I was getting words of encouragement from some members, and others were not for it. I wasn't worried though because once God gave the go ahead then that's all that matters. Doing the will of the father.

I got married in my early thirties, and I thought then, "Yes, I escape the relationship rejections." Not long after I got married, I got pregnant. I was happy. I was mindful that this is a new marriage, and I must work hard to be a good wife and an upcoming mom. The twins were born eight months premature, due to preeclampsia. My husband and I had another situation to face. One of the twin Javon had an issue with his heart. I never feared though. A week prior to the emergency cesarean section, the Holy Spirit woke me up at 6:00 a.m. and warned me of this to come. The spirit of the Lord said, "I am a giver of good gifts, let not your heart be troubled, and the doctor's will be confounded." I watched and saw God's mighty hands moved in this situation.

Today, he is doing great. Life as we know it was pretty busy. Being a full-time wife, mother, pastor, and worker was hard, but I was very committed to the task. Every day I rose to the challenge and try to be as productive as God would help me to be. I would just believe that as I lived holy and be the Proverbs-Chapter-Thirty-One woman that the Bible talked about that things would be well. I was wrong! oh, so wrong. The enemy showed his ugly head and went after the weaker vessel, my husband.

My husband's family is blessed with the gift of music. I mean the Lord used them in an awesome way. They all know how to play multiple musical instrument. They are always playing at church events, sometimes together or other times individually. It would not be strange or out of place if he comes to me and said he has to play at a function. It is not every day or every week, but when the opportunity arise, I never got in his way. Remember, he wasn't working full time, and any additional income was welcome. I never had any reason to think that he was unfaithful. Everything that he did was well-hidden behind the music. I helped him, and now, he was a resident of the United States. I even got him a job at the hospital where I worked.

One Sunday, while I was home on maternity leave, I received a phone call from one of my church sister, and she asked if I was okay. Not that anything was wrong with the question, but the Holy Spirit bore witness that something wasn't right. I was to later found out that my husband's name was being called up with one of the young lady in the church. I was sick on the inside. I was home recovering from the C-section and take care of the twins Jayden and Javon. I was also dealing with the high blood pressure and the pain from the surgery. I prayed and asked God to intervene and to allow me to know the truth. The young lady was pregnant, and they were saying he might be the father. She did give birth, and when it was time to dedicate her baby, I had already asked God to please spare me and let the real father show up. God answered me; the baby's father was present, but that didn't exclude the fact that his name was called. The one thing that was true: my husband's genes is very strong, and once you see his children, you see him. He might have escape this one, but it still left a scar upon my heart.

I confronted my husband who did nothing more than deny, deny, deny. I told him if the marriage is not what he wants, then to let us get a divorce. I didn't get married to get a divorce, so I told him that I don't want any mess, and if he feels as though he doesn't want the marriage, then let it be dissolved in a decent way. I really don't like scandal and back and forth. I lived a life where I would pray if I hear something that was not good. I honestly do not spread stories. I always live by: love covers a multitude of sin. Pray and work on whatever needed to be in line with the will of God.

It was my life on the screen for the whole church to see. He said, "Nad, I don't want that to happen to our family." I was very embarrassed. I am the kind of person who believed and lived a life that private things must stay private. But what do you do when your private pain becomes public? The church family was talking about you, and they all had their version of the story. I lifted my head up and kept pressing on. I never played the naive Christian. I was deeply aware and concerned that trouble has walked through my door and hit the marriage. I kept my guard up. The thing that got me was that people never thought that we would make it when we got married. Therefore, to see this happening was truly devastating.

I lived life as an intercessor. I prayed for people. I prayed for my church family all the time. I often wondered: Is anyone praying for me? Did anyone lift up a prayer asking God to help this young family? It was months later that I began to notice that he began to distance himself by making himself as busy as possible. I never said anything right away because I didn't want to come across as a nagging wife. I just kept on trusting that as we take it one day at a time, we will have a breakthrough. I now realized that sometimes in not saying anything was like ignoring the elephant in the room.

I never made him feel less than a man. I encouraged him on almost every idea he wanted to pursue. I encouraged him to go to college and enhance his education. I helped him with his school work when he needed me to. I truly believed in working together to better each other and the family. If something didn't sit well, I would state my opinion, but there were never any fights or quarreling in or outside of the house. If one of us was upset, we always tried to talk it out. Also, one of us always stayed silent and allowed the other to state the issues or concerns at hand. I trusted God and was willing to try and make the family work. If I was single, I would have run faster than the road runner. I thought about the children and also the fact that I am not a quitter.

One day, I wrote him a letter to explain to him that he has distanced himself from me and the children. I was sitting on the bed while he was getting dressed to leave. I wish I could erase the memory. He picked up the letter glanced over it and put it down. It registered in my heart that day that he was already gone mentally. He was only here in body, and it won't be too long before the body followed him to where his heart and mind is. Eventually things kept deteriorating. I was working overtime to keep it together. But it was hopeless because he wasn't willing to work it out. I didn't want my family to know that I was hurting. Also, I didn't want my coworkers to know that I was unhappy.

The funny thing was I started wearing makeup to work. Just a little to brighten my face. I am so not a makeup person. Now that I think about it, I can laugh because I kept on getting compliments that I look nice. I didn't feel nice though. I wanted to scream, but the sound wouldn't come if I tried. I didn't want the inside to show up on the outside. I carried on with my work as usual, always giving my all. I was a very dedicated worker. So I poured out everything that I had into the job, and when I came home, I made it my mission to keep my children contented. I kept on telling myself that I can't ignore the obvious, and it was quite hard to wrap my mind about what I had expected life to be and what it is. It felt like the bottom had fallen out, and no end was in sight.

CHAPTER 2

The Word Before the Storm

In March of 2011, I just got home from work when I received a phone call from an evangelist that I knew. She asked me if I was praying for my husband's job? I answered yes. She said the Lord said to tell me that he is the one who has blocked him. I was shocked. I really was praying for him to get a part-time or full-time position. He was only working per diem. She went on to tell me that God has some other things that he wants to say to him. I told her he wasn't home because he worked the overnight shift but hold everything, and we will come to see her at an appointed time. We got there, and then she explained everything the Lord had showed her about him. Basically, the Lord pleaded with him to get his life in order. She also touched on private conversation that only him and I had. The Holy Spirit revealed to the evangelist that if my husband surrendered to God's will, how God was going to use him mightily, and the abundance of blessings he was going to pour out on him and us as a family. I knew God really loves us and has sent us help. But he didn't take God up on his offer.

He didn't take heed to the warning, and so I continued to pray, and God continued to reveal the hidden things. It was April 24, 2011, I was scheduled to moderate the Easter service. That Saturday, he said he had to go to track and field competition; he was on the team at the college he attended. I was soon to find out that he was lying. It got late, so I called him but no response. I lay on my bed, and then in the realm of the spirit, I saw a phone number flashed before my eyes. I can't explain it to you because I never saw it before. I have seen things in the spirit before but never a phone number. I got up and picked up my phone to see a text message from him. I looked at the text and knew that it wasn't written by my husband. Being around someone, you get to learn their language even in writing. I also had seen a text from a strange phone number.

I answered the text, and the person on the other end just kept lying. The person's text begins with "babe." My husband never called me babe. He called me "Nad," short for Nadine. However, I wasn't playing the game, so I tried his phone a few more times but no answer. It was almost 5:00 a.m., Easter Sunday morning when he called back. Knowing that he was busted, as cold as ice, this was what he said, "Nad, for whatever it's worth, I am sorry." It was like my world crashed. Someone has pulled the rug out from under my feet. My feet got weak, and I began to cry. I called my best friend at that time and cried; and then I was finally able to tell her why I am interrupting her life so early in the morning.

He came home the morning I told him that it was too late to call the church and cancel because he was the musician scheduled to play that morning. I actually told him to ask God for forgiveness and play the service. Looking back, I know that was wrong. I went to church and moderated the service. The power of God was in the house as I brought God's people into his presence. All the while my heart was shattered into fifty million pieces. I made it through the day. I was lost in thoughts, trying to figure out how fragile life is. Your world can fall apart in a twinkling of an eye. I wanted to make sure that even in this mess, I walked circumspectly. I wanted to handle this crisis in the best way.

I asked him further on in the week after I gathered my thoughts if he wants his family and what does he plan to do. He said yes, he wanted his family. I remember saying to him, "You need to read this," and I handed him the Bible which was opened to psalm 51. He did read it, but he was not like David; he wasn't broken in his spirit. I told him I'm so disappointed and it is going to be very difficult, but we can go seek counseling. He agreed, but it never happened. I decided that I wasn't going to force him. Neither was I going to beg him to love me or even to stay. He kept living his dirty lifestyle. I stayed at my parent's house while he stayed in the apartment.

It was now May, and prior to finding about his affair, the family was booked to go on vacation in Jamaica. He still wanted to come, and so we went. But we lived like brother and sister. Both him and I deserved an Oscar award for best actor and supporting actress. No one in my family knew of our troubles. He even wore his wedding band that he hardly wore when we were home in the states. I have lots of uncles and male cousins, and if they had found out that I wasn't happy, they would have put an unholy Jamaican beating on him. I didn't want to be responsible for that, so I played the role real well. After our time was up, we came back to the states. Life was never the same. He wanted his cake and also be able to eat it too. He wanted the security of a family and also to be a player. He was wavering, and I wasn't going to be tossed about like I don't know what time it was. He was between two opinions. He seemed to have wanted his family, but something was pulling him back to the other side. He had no complaints because I asked him to tell me if I needed to do anything different. He left me one night when I was helping him in writing a paper and taking care of the twins. He said he had to leave to take a suitcase to one of his friend who was travelling the next day. I know he was lying, and he was going to see the other woman. As I sat there typing the paper that he received an A on, he was failing miserably at saving his marriage.

CHAPTER 3

The Storm

In June of the same year, we were talking, and on the nineteenth of that month, we were together as man and wife for the last time. I still don't know how it happened. We did the laundry together and was talking, and after that, we were together. A few days or so after that, he came by my parent's house, and the baby was sleeping on the bed. He was wearing a blue jeans and a light-blue polo shirt. He leaned up against the dresser in the room. Then out came words of rejection in all its various forms of the definition. He said, "If I could feel for you half of what I feel for this girl, then I would stay, but I don't."

The words hit my heart like someone was literally stabbing me. It was one of the worst pains ever. I picked up my baby and walked outside into the backyard. I sat on the swing and tears just started to gush out without my ability to hold them back. I was rejected! I thought about how I tried my best to be a good wife to him. I really did. The house was a home. The children were always taken care of. His needs were always met. I supported him in every way I know how. I prayed for him a whole lot, sometimes more than I did for myself. I knew then and there that my life had turned and such darkness overshadowed my skies. He doesn't want me. He didn't fight for me or his children. There is no hero coming to my rescue in this situation. My life flashed before my eyes. I put up with a whole lot, and this is the thanks I get. I felt like he was saying, "No thanks for being a good woman." I felt the bitter echo of thanks for being a fool. I also heard the echoes of the church members saying, "I told you it wasn't going to work." It hurt a whole lot. I loved him, but he has made it clear that he doesn't love me.

Suddenly, after three and a half years of marriage, it was over just like that. It was what people said, that we wouldn't make it. He didn't try one bit to save his family. The greener grass called, and he answered. But as they say, "the grass is not always greener on the other side." By now, I came to find out that this girl was his math tutor in college. Ironic, isn't it? I encouraged him to go back to school, and instead of coming out as a licensed registered nurse, he came out with Candice. One day she called first, she asked if the 2009 Toyota Camry was his. I answered, last time I check the car is in my name. But I wasn't ready for the ultimate rejection. She asked if the children was his. She said, he denies being their father. I told the young lady to lose my number, and I went as far as to change my number. I realized that he left a wife for a plaything. She was more interested in what he had than who he is.

You don't know how the mind deals with such rejection. On one hand, he doesn't want you, and that's one thing to deal with. But how do you deal with the fact that he's turning his back on his children. He knows I am a clean woman. I never cheated and try to pass off the children as his. He is inferring that I'm like him. I took my marriage wows seriously. I was all for my marriage and family. How dare him, all of this for sex? Or new love? This kind of rejection took me to a new low. I was hurting very badly. I was in a few days of fasting when the Holy Spirit instructed me to take the car from him. I asked for the key, and as I drove off, I asked the Holy Spirit where should I go? I drove a few blocks away from the house and parked under a tree. I said, Holy Ghost what am I looking for? I began to search the glove compartment but nothing unusual.

Then the spirit of the Lord directed me to the back pockets on both seats. I found seven pennies in a bag. They were painted red, blue, and purple. In the other pocket was a handkerchief. Instantly, I was overcome by a force; I couldn't see for a few minutes. I began calling on the name of Jesus and pleading the blood of Jesus. One night, I went to midweek service, and I asked the bishop to pray for him. I brought the things to the church and showed it to the brethren. The statement was made that maybe they were in the car before we bought it. But unless Toyota is using unknown force to sell a brand-new car then I would agree. I kept everything in as best as I could but never say never. It was June 23, 2011, it was the twin's third birthday that my emotions burst open like a shaken can of soda. I was shaken too much, and I was about to explode.

He came to my parents' house, and he wanted his passport. I was not in a hurry to give it to him. He was going to Jamaica to visit one of his women down there. We went back and forth for a little, and then I just stayed silent. I didn't move fast enough to give him the passport, so he called the police. Then somehow he came into the hallway by the bedroom. I faced him, and I asked him, "What make you wicked so!" (This was straight up Jamaican slang.) I drew my right hand back and slapped him in the face. I swore I heard a heavenly choir sang. I heard *ahhhhh*. I continued to slap him on his chest like a school girl fighting. My mother was present, and as I kept repeating this to him and still hitting him in the chest, I heard my mother started to cry. She asked him, "Did you really hurt Nadine?" She came in between the two of us, and that's when I came to myself and walked away. I went into the bathroom, took a shower, packed up the kids, and left the house. I never ever had put my hand on a man before. He never put his hand on me ever. I couldn't believe that the pain of rejection brought me so low. My greatest fear has become my reality. I left with the children, and I pulled off just as the cops was driving up.

I went to a girlfriend of mine in Long Island. I repeated the Bible that I know and kept on encouraging myself. I was in shock. I didn't know what to do. How am I going to make it? I am about to be a single mother of three children. I cried out to Jesus. How could this be happening to me? What have I done to deserve this? I wasn't in a rush to get married. I waited on you. I was very helpful and was never jealous of neither friends or family who was getting married. I expected this to work. What has gone wrong? Remember, I didn't really lived because I didn't want to be rejected. Then the classic, why God? Why me? I laid everything down at God's feet. I kept praying what seemed to be like every hour. I know I needed a whole ton load of strength.

I began to ask God why me. If you love me, how could you let this happen to me. I didn't live a crazy life. I wanted the marriage and family life. I had run from other prospect because I wanted to make sure God was in my choice. I thought about the shame, the church, and everything possible. I felt like I failed. I went through the process over and over in my head. How did I ended up here? This is not what I wanted. I was put aside. Like Job, the thing that I feared the most has come upon me. I went from married to a single mother, faster than a speeding bullet.

It was at this point I had to decide if I am going to let this degree of rejection kill my spirit or turn me into someone I'm not. You may have asked yourself the question did I ever saw any clues. I would give you an honest answer, no. You see, he is a musician, and he worked the overnight shift. He plays at concerts and other church functions. He would hide his deeds behind this fact. It wasn't strange for him to say he has a function tonight. I would have responded okay. I was his wife, not a lo-jack. I never asked where, what, when, and why. I trusted him, that he would do what is right for his family. As mentioned before, I realized that when some men cheat they leave clues, but he hid it in the things of God, and that is why God exposed him. I trusted my husband. We were both serving the Lord. I never believed in keeping tabs on any grown up. Relationship must be built on trust as one of the key factors. It was later on, as the Lord began to remove the veil, that I was able to see much clearer.

I came to realize that God will take you up on your offer to serve him fully. You see, I said, "I'm yours, Lord, use me, Lord," and other famous words of commitment we say as Christians. How could God asked me to do something that he knew was not going to work. In the Bible, I knew of the story of Hosea, Samson, and in Judges chapter twenty, where the king inquired of God if they should battle against their brethren, the tribe of Benjamin, and the Lord said yes. Israel went up against them twice, and they were beaten sorely. They spent the whole day in fasting and inquiring of the Lord, that was when God gave them the victory. I couldn't tell anyone any of this.

If God was in it, it should have worked? But just like in this battle, marriage is work. We get out of it what we put into it. I pause here for a moment to tell somebody that sometimes God will require you to do something, and you will come out looking like a loser but stand still, God is in control. I asked him one day, "Why did you marry me?" He answered and said, "I marry you because I didn't want a girl, I wanted a wife. I chose you because you are wife quality." Now this was his confession. Now he could never go to God and accuse God of never providing him a wife. God is no man's debtor. His ways are far from finding out. He is God alone, and as Eli says to Samuel years ago, "He is God, and he does whatsoever He pleases."

No one was telling me anything, not even his best friends. I went into a lot of fasting and prayer, and that's how I began to learn a lot of things to the point where he started to tell on himself. One night, we were coming from Tuesday night service at the church, and he said to me, "You see, when I told you that I was going to some of the functions, I went to parties instead. I drink." I reached out to one of his closest friends and asked him if the above was true. He wasn't so forthcoming, but he respected me, and finally he said yes; but he felt like it wasn't his place to say anything.

Another example was in the basement of my parents' house; he had hidden a black duffel bag. My mother and one of my nephew was cleaning up the basement when my nephew came across it. The bag was full with pornography tapes, pictures of women's private parts, a big bag of condoms and letters. I went through the whole bag, and I was going to dump it into the garbage bin we rented for the trash removal, but I didn't. I in turn took it and showed it to my closest friend at the time as evidence to show that I'm not lying on him, or I left him without a cause. It was the hardest thing I ever had to do.

Well then, so I thought. Presented with all the evidence and also knowing that the girl whose name he was called with wasn't the beginning, neither the countless others that was evident in the bag. I had to make an appointment at my gynecologist office because I was scared. I walked in the morning of my appointment and told my doctor to run every possible sexually transmitted disease, and he did.

I was so nervous because I didn't know what to expect, but thanks be to God, they all came back negative.

I got up one morning and went over to the apartment. It was shocking; the place looked bad, and it seemed as if he was not living there. I packed up everything that I could take for myself and the kids. I called my best friend at the time to come for some of the furniture. I never looked back. Had it not been for my parents, I probably would have been homeless.

I have to now face and deal with my new reality. I took all of the Bible that I knew and tell myself that God will not give me more than I could bear. Even though I felt the weight from the pressure of the situation, I poured out my heart before him. I was angry like the Bible says, but somehow I can't really explain it. I didn't lose it. I didn't end up in a psych ward. God kept me, and he never let me go. It was strange for the months following. The only communication we had from then on was only when he was to spend time with the children. I had gone to the bishop and told him I wanted to meet with him. I brought the Evangelist that the Lord sent to talk to him in 2011. In that meeting, the same Evangelist said, "Is it possible that I heard from God, but she moved too quickly to marry him." I was floored. "I felt like she was questioning the timing of the marriage." I left the meeting feeling very sad and downcast. I told bishop and first lady later on that I will be taking three months off to be there for my children. I also didn't want to be there to see the pity or anything else that the people in the church will offer. I was contemplating not going back to church. I literally was walking in the valley of the shadow of death. I remember that the bishop and his wife came by my house to check on me. They both talked, encouraged, and prayed with me. However, I would never forget the words of my first lady, she said, "You have nothing to worry about. You are a woman of integrity." These words meant the world to me. It somehow helped to lift a bit of the shame I felt.

I didn't tell anyone that I was divorced except my family and a close friend. I received a call from the Evangelist she wanted to know how was things. I said I'm good. She began to tell me that she saw my ex-husband going after a young woman in the church where she was.

I told her he was free to do whatever he wanted to do. She was taken by surprise at my response. She asked me what do I mean? I then let her in on the secret I carried, "We are officially divorce." We spoke a little bit, and then she began to pray. God had her confess that I did hear from God, and the married was ordained by God, but he was the one who messed it up. I smiled after the call ended. God has a sense of humor. I am very careful to not say God said, if he didn't. I do not fear man. I truly reverence God.

Exactly ten months after June 23 episode, I got a phone call from him in April 2012. He said he was at the post office mailing me my copy of the divorce paper. It was now official. This man got rid of me faster than you could even blink. I didn't want to die physically, but I wanted to die spiritually.

Later on toward the end of the year, the enemy set up an opportunity for me to do it. I would commit a sin, and God must and have to turn his back on me. It is hard to believe that after reading and knowing that I could never fall so far that God would ever leave me. Yet the pain in the midst of the situation spoke out louder than the facts that I knew. The psalmist David said, "If I make my bed even in hell, thou art there." In the situation, the Lord showed up, stopped the process, and said, "Not even spiritual suicide, I wouldn't allow you to commit." I needed attention, and the devil knew I didn't get any at all from the one person that I expected it from, and that was the man I had married. I was able to look the devil in the face and tell him that I will not allow him to use me to help him destroy me. I was grateful for all the grace and mercy that God gave me.

Things just kept on getting worse and worse. I would love to tell you that I saw the light at the end of the tunnel. It was as dark as it could be. I was living from paycheck to paycheck. So I already know that financially I was in a whole lot of trouble. I filed for bankruptcy. I had to voluntarily have my car repossessed. I lost everything. I didn't even had money to buy a bottle of milk. But truth be told, I kept on praying. That was all I knew, and it was my calm in this treacherous storm.

The pain of separation for the twins who were three at the time was very hard. My baby girl was six months old. She didn't feel it as such. The twins cried for two years straight. There were nights I asked God to just let his spirit sweep over them so that they would go to sleep. The pain of separation that they felt was expressed in their tears. I would stay up with them, hold them, and comforted them until they went to sleep. I was exhausted working ten-and twelve-hour shift and coming home to hurting kids. I am truly amazed that I did not lost my mind. Can I just interject here to say: God is a keeper.

CHAPTER 4

Breaking Day

It has been a long road, but day after day and night after night, I sought the Lord. It is very important to listen and do what the spirit of the Lord bids us to do. Before I even met him and got married, my daily walk with God was constant. He told me to go into fasting in 2005. Fasting is a time that one takes to deny his or herself food and just go after God. During this time, you are drawing closer to God. It's not just the giving up of the food, but time spent reading his words and praying fervently. I with my smart self answered the Holy Spirit and said, "But I fast." The Lord was calling me to a higher level. I never did twenty-one days of fasting before. I listened to Jentezen Franklin, bought his fasting book, and set out for this period of fasting. You see, what the Lord was doing was helping me to build up strength in the spirit. He alone knows what's ahead of us.

I read God's word and keep on doing what I can do every day for my children. It was hard and rough. There were days I felt like Elijah under the juniper tree. But there was always someone, or the Holy Spirit pulling me along. I couldn't die in this process. I have to make it through. I'm counting on me. My children are counting on me, and most importantly God is counting on me. I have a story. I have a testimony. You will not die in the process. Depression cannot control you in the process. If you lie down and die and live in pity-party land, then and only then depression and despair will overtake you. We have to sit the test, though it may be hard, rough, and overwhelming at times. We have to press on because we overcome by the blood of the lamb and by the word of our testimonies.

God used his people to bless and to encourage me also. Sometimes the very item I needed to get for the children, God would have someone buy it for them. One day, I went into a variety store, and they had a Dora the Explorer backpack for $5.99. And I thought to myself, my Jazzy would love this bag, but I couldn't buy it because I didn't have any money at all. I cried and came home and went into my room. My mother knocked on the door and told me she was going out and will be back soon. Later on, she came back and handed me a black plastic bag. She said I saw this and thought of Jazzy. It was the same bag that I couldn't afford. God allowed her to buy it for me. Listen, this is the honest truth. I never told her because I was ashamed that I couldn't provide something so simple for my child.

He knows the things that we are in need of, and while we are asking him, he's answering as the Bible says. You don't need a lot of people; you need only a faithful few. After a few years have passed, I found out that people were praying for me. They never said it then, but I was happy to know. I learned something from this. Please pray one for the other, and every now and then, let someone know that you are praying for them. It does help a lot. I lived to see my ex-husband telling everyone he meets and introduced me to, that I'm the best woman he knows. I literally had to tell him to stop it. If I am who you say I am, then how is it that you walked away.

I also lived to hear him come back and testify how all the blessings God wanted him to have, which was revealed by the Evangelist in 2011 passed him by. He would be playing for a well-known church, getting a stipend that would have taken care of the bills and enough remaining to take care of anything we needed, just like the Lord said. He also came and confessed to me that the hot love had died, and the girl wasn't who he thought she was. You see, God doesn't like ugly. While he was playing me, he got played. Everything he did to me, she did it back to him. I don't know if he thought that I would feel sorry for him because we have a saying, "if you make your bed then lie down in it." On one of his visit with the children, we were sitting at the kitchen table when he shook his head and said, "Boy, Nad, you were with me, for me, and not for anything I had." I laughed and asked what brought this on. He said he doesn't know, but life is just not working out the way he had hoped.

It is very important to practice what we preach. God will test you while you are in the storm. In 2011, after he had left, he was still on my insurance at work because we did the yearly renewal in December for January of the new year. He called me one day to get some information. To tell you the truth, I didn't want to talk to him, but sitting at the desk, I heard the voice of God said so clearly, "Do not repay evil with evil, but overcome evil with good." He wanted the insurance information to make an appointment for himself. I gave him everything. I made up in my mind that I will do whatever I can to have a peaceful relationship with him because God wants me to, and I didn't want to cause any unnecessary pain for my children. Also, nothing that I could do would ever compare to the hand of God moving against him.

I also prayed and asked God to take away every hurt and pain. Help me to forgive him. I didn't want any bitterness in my heart. I read in the Psalms that if I have iniquity in my heart then the Lord will not hear me. I needed God to hear me so I live peaceable with him. I had to heal. I made up in my mind that I would not be bitter, I would be better. I just took it one day at a time.

He remembered the power and effectiveness of the prayers that I prayed for him before. In September 2016, I was in my room; the phone rang. It was my ex-husband calling for me to pray that he gets into one of the government jobs that he applied for. He has been waiting for a very long time and no answer up until he reached out to me. I lifted up a prayer for him, and we said goodbye. It was half an hour later, he called me back overjoyed because New York corrections called him. God has a sense of humor, then the police department and the firefighter called him as well. I just smiled. I love God with all my heart. I just looked up to heaven and said, "You did it again. All praise and glory belong to you." He was so grateful. He told me thanks for praying for him.

It was during this time of his job processing that he called me and was telling me about all he has to go through for this job. He then said to me when he went through the psychological evaluation that he told the psychologist that I am his best friend. I smiled once again. It was November third when he called me and asked me if I would give him another chance. I told him no. By now, the Lord had revealed so much that I really have to be honest if he had chosen his family in the beginning then I would have given him another chance, and maybe we would have made it. I have matured and moved on from the rejection, and I don't know if I would be able to trust him again.

The devil would have wanted to capture me and play the rejection over and over until I sink into deep depression. The reason being the finding out of his affair came to light on one of the most sacred days on the Christian calendar, Easter Sunday. So every Easter Sunday, I am reminded of that event. Also, I have to remember on the twin's birthday every June 23 that it was a fateful day like this that their father walked out on the entire family. The memories will always remind you. One Christmas after the divorce, my eldest sister and one of our brothers-in-law were talking, and it was about marriages. I heard my sister laughed out loud and said, "I have never seen anyone treated a man as good as Nadine, not even me." The truth was setting me free while at the same time, reminding me that I failed even though I tried my best. My own sister was testifying of how committed a wife I was to him. So memory was reminding me because my marriage was over. It is what you do at these critical time that will help you to continue to move on or to wallow in self-pity. But God! I have to take a praise break. Hallelujah, thank you Jesus, for sustaining grace. Oh, how I bless his name. If the enemy shows up with his pity-party record, Jesus shows up with a word or a song.

It is so important to stay in the word. When things are good and when things are bad, stay connected to God. He is the only one that can carry you when you can't even carry yourself. He becomes your everything. Oh, how I learn to lean and depend on Jesus. I would have lost my mind had it not been for my relationship with God. Don't play church, my brothers and sisters. Be an authentic, genuine believer. Be truthful and honest in all that you do. It is the master that will carry you through. No matter what happens to you, get up, my God, dust off yourself and take up your cross and follow him because he will lead you beside the still waters.

No one wants to go through like that. No one plans a future to watch it go up in smoke so to speak. No one wants to be rejected. It does something to you. Your emotions immediately pick up on it, and it's like the feel-bad chemicals start mixing up inside of you, and you just feel so bad. But God has a purpose for our lives. Nothing that happens to us is a surprise to him. Remember he knows our end from the beginning. It is the messy middle we really don't know about. But the God who allowed you to enter this earth realm is the same God who is going to finish your course. You have to speak to yourself. Tell yourself it cannot end like this. I am a winner, and a winner never quits. You have to keep on fighting. You can't give in to emotions or negative people. Yes, cry if you have to, but dry your eyes and gather yourself. Tell the devil I have cried enough over this situation, and that you have cried your last tears of sorrow. You are going to make it to the days when the tears flowing will be tears of joy. Preach to yourself like David did, "Soul, why are you cast down, hope thou in God." For I shall yet praise him who is the health of my countenance and my God. God is our very present help in times of trouble.

Listen to as much worship music and sermons as possible. I use my break time on the job. I lock myself in the supply storage room. I listen to sermons, especially "God of My Tight Place" by T. D. Jakes. I make up worship songs as I worship God. I had to stay strong. This doesn't take away from your personal devotion time with God, but it helps. You have to constantly keep your heart and mind stayed upon Jesus. I realized if you don't hold onto or better yet, let God hold you, then one slip and you will fall into utter sadness. You can't allow this because the Bible says the joy of the Lord is our strength. The word of God quickens you and I. When it gets into our spirit and soul, it's like a geyser out of our bellies, rivers of living water gushes out. The Lord knows we are built to last. We shall not die but live and declare the works of God. You and I are going through, not because of us, but because of who will cross our path, and we will have the words of life to speak into their lives.

I couldn't die physically, emotionally, or spiritually. Remember I am a pastor. I served in my local church. It is during this time; I was promoted to second associate pastor. I used to sing on the worship team, moderate church services, and just be available for the master's use in the kingdom. Moreover, God's people were depending on me. I had to always be ready to pray when my phone rings, and the voice on the other end says, "Pastor, please pray for me." It doesn't matter how I get the requests I always prayed. I believe that in doing this, attending to others' needs, I couldn't spend too much time on my mess. In praying, it kept the fire burning constantly on the altar. I was receiving fresh strength even when it didn't even felt like it.

The next level or dimension always costs a price. I didn't even know that I was being considered for this position. It came as a complete shock. You never know what God is up to, and if you could be like a child and just trust him, you and I may not understand why we must go this way. But be assured that God walks with us, and he talks with us. He is leading us along. The good old song says, "In shady green pastures so rich and so sweet, God leads his dear children along, where the water cools flows bathed the weary one feet God leads his dear children along. Some through the waters, some through the flood, some through fire, but all through the blood. Some through great sorrows, but God gives a song in the night season and all the day long."

CHAPTER 5

The Power of Prayer

It is very important that as a child of God, we develop a strong prayer life. I am always praying. I literally call upon the Lord every opportunity that I get. The prayer life that I had before I got married only increased after I got married. This was key because I always kept sending up prayer for my family and anyone who called upon me and those the Lord laid on my heart. I had a book that I wrote that was full of prayers that I pray after I had prayed until I couldn't anymore; I began to write prayers to the Lord about my husband at the time. One day, I got so mad that I began to rip out the pages of all the prayer I had written about him. It was when there were no more pages, and as I stood there looking at the empty book, only the cover in my hands; I then realized and to quote the line from *Diary of a Mad Black Women*, "I prayed for him, more than I had prayed for myself." The days when I couldn't see my way, I prayed. I would work a ten- to twelve-hour shift and came home to my children. That was so sad. I did all that I could do. I hugged them and rocked them to sleep and prayed for them continuously. Oh, God, I would cry, heal my babies' broken hearts!

I am an intercessor. I go to God on behalf of others. I literally take on the situation as if it was my own, and I pray it through until the person gets an answer or a breakthrough. It wasn't easy to stand in the gap for myself and my children when my heart was broken into so many pieces. But every day, it seemed like, after the night had passed, I woke up with just enough strength to make it through the next day. Prayer was all I knew. So I prayed day in, day out, nonstop.

It was also necessary for me to pray back to God what he has said in his words. There were days I would pray, "Lord, if it's possible, please let this cup pass from me." I would pray, "Lord, you promised that you won't give me more than I can bear." There were days I felt like Brother Job, "Though you slay me yet will I trust you." Then I would turn like Brother Moses and cry, "O Lord, though art my dwelling place. It is your words that You have caused me thy servant to hope upon. You promised that when I am forsaken, then you oh Lord will take me up." I prayed until words fail me and the tears flow and the groaning that cannot be uttered takes over.

The one thing I never did was to stop praying. I knew where my strength comes from, and I called upon the Lord always. The Bible says, "Men are always to pray and not faint." Therefore, though physically I felt weak, spiritually I was putting on pure muscle. I fully comprehend the scripture that says, we must "pray without ceasing."

It is very vital that you don't let the pain cause you to stop calling out to God. Satan will whisper thoughts that are designed to make and keep you depressed. Not long after he starts talking, you find yourself agreeing with the adversary. I had questions. I doubted myself. I asked myself, Nadine, did you really hear from God? Surely, if God said yes, then how come this mess. Why didn't the marriage work? I was a good wife, and I'm not just saying it. I really was. I watched my mom take care of my dad, and I followed what I saw. The home is always well kept. The house is a home, not a hostile environment. To all that I saw, I put Proverbs 31 in the mix, and that was how I had my home. I even asked him one day, "Is there anything that I'm not doing as a wife? We should talk about it." He answered, me saying all was well.

It was even harder when the church, which I was attending from top to bottom, felt like no support. I only got the pity steers and the silent, "I told you so." I couldn't even say: "I know God had given me the okay. Look at Brother Hosea wasn't that God." His marriage didn't look like what he wanted it to be. I was in a difficult place, so I had to hold on to the one thing that I know to be the proven weapon and that is prayer. No matter what is happening or has happened. Do not take prayer out of the mix. Prayer line to heaven will never be busy unless you decided that you're not ringing on and on. Remember Brother James said, "The effectual fervent prayer of the righteous availeth much."

There will be time when you can't enter into a deep prayer; where you pray, and you know and felt like something has happened. This is where you have to manage your emotions and trust God. If you have to do like blind Bartimaeaus, and cry, "Jesus, son of David, have mercy upon me." Then that's the prayer you pray. Lord, help me, I don't know what to do, then pray that. It is critical to put into the prayer reservoir as much as you can so when dark days appear, you can make a withdrawal. Finally, pray the Lord's Prayer; after all, that is the model Jesus gave to his disciples. If it is so grim that none of the above comes to mind, then when you don't have the words to pray, just say Lord help me.

CHAPTER 6

Forgiveness

Forgiveness is the key in helping you to let go of the baggage called hurt. The dictionary defined forgiveness as "the intentional and voluntary process by which a person undergoes a change in feelings and attitude regarding an offense, lets go of negative emotions such as vengefulness, with an increased ability to wish the offender well." This is a mouthful, but it is so true. I was angry and upset for a few months right after the breakdown of the marriage. I didn't want to see him. I needed to think. I also wanted to make sure that I didn't seek revenge. I didn't let anger and bitterness consume me. I quickly sought the help of the Holy Spirit and got my act together. I read a quote by Marianne Williamson which states, "Unforgiveness is like drinking poison and hoping the other person would die."

I accepted the fact that he didn't want me. I told myself to come to grips with this reality. I also saw evidences that he didn't want me because he went to live with this young woman to whom he said he loves a lot. I then came up with a plan to have him call the children using my mother's landline. He wasn't doing it 100 percent, but I was happy that the children could speak with him. I then suggested that he comes and takes them maybe to breakfast or wherever he chooses as long as he stays in touch with me. It didn't happen overnight because he always kept himself busy, so most of the time, he has to fit them into his schedule. But I kept at it. By this time, the twins were four years old, and my daughter was two years old. One day, he came, and this was the first time my daughter saw him in a long time. He said hi to her, and she ran away and held onto me.

I have power. I could use this against him. What would you do? This was a perfect opportunity for me to let the spirit of revenge come alive, and to let unforgiveness thrive, but I chose to kill it immediately and insisted that my daughter give him a hug and say hi. I kept him abreast of all their activities. It was up to him to come if he wanted to or not. I never used my children as pawns or set any obstacle in his way. I made up in my mind that I wasn't going to use my children to spite a guy who has hurt me. I never gave him any room whatsoever to point his finger at me and said I have been unfair.

To this day, he still has a problem putting the children first. He needs to totally surrender his life to Christ so that the Lord can help him with his weaknesses. As I am writing this book, he has already divorced his third wife. I don't get involved in his personal life. He's the one who tells me this information. I don't try to find out anything about him. My primary concern is that he shows up when he's to get the children. He takes care of them when they are with him. I just remind him nicely that they are growing up. Presently, the twins are ten, and my daughter is eight. So I have held his hands this far, and I told him the other day: The children are growing up and it is up to him how he wants his children to see him. Always remember that the children are innocent in all of this, and you don't want to do anything to add any extra pain to their broken, wounded heart. Even though you yourself are hurting, numb your pain and allow God to heal you while you apply healing to your child or children as well.

My advice to any hurting women. Don't let your emotions rule you when you are in a crisis. Manage your emotions and do it well. Let sound reasoning and judgement be your guide. Date a lot more than I did. Get to know the person who you are planning to spend the rest of your life with. Forgive yourself and move your life along. Live your life in such a way that you yourself don't have to tell people anything. As you walk circumspectly, let him tell others the kind of woman you are. I literally had to beg my ex-husband to stop telling people how wonderful I am. Be fair in all that you do, but also be aware if you recognized that your ex is taking advantage of you.

Remember that God will always be true and every man a liar. There was a part of the warning that the evangelist had given us. It was that he was going to come back to me someday and ask for me to take him back, which he did. She had also confirmed that I had heard from God; and because I followed the biding of the Lord, God is going to bless me. I chose to let go and let God. I pray you do the same. God can restore broken marriages; I totally believe that he can. He also will walk with you as you try very hard to pick up the broken pieces and go on your separate ways. Pray, "Forgive my debts as I forgive those who trespass against me. Deliver me from all evil. For thine is the kingdom, the power, and the glory forever and ever. Amen."

CHAPTER 7

Healing Rain

Every day, I try to forgive myself for allowing the enemy to make me feel like a fool. I also came to grips with the fact that his short comings and his sin wasn't my cross to carry. I loved someone who through all of his ways showed me that he didn't love me. I looked at my situation and do a total assessment. I really asked myself if holding on to anger or if I let bitterness come into my heart, what would I gain. I made sure that the children were always available when he wants them, but he stayed away for a while. I never spoke anything negative about him around them. I kept it as clear and sane as possible.

It was out of this pain that a deeper understanding of my ministry was birthed. It was after I have been through the rejection that my prayer life of intercession for marriages and family increased. I was able to put on my evaluation sheet as I was studying to become an ordained minister that I am called to help God's people but especially hurting women. I am not the first to have been rejected, and I won't be the last. I know though that I can minister to hurting women because I am touched with the feelings of their infirmity. I would be able to connect to people because I have walked this road. I've been there. I know the loneliness. I know what it feels like to long for the affection from your spouse but got nothing in return. I know what it's like to feel all alone even though you are in a marriage.

It was a few months after my fast in 2016 when I woke up and heard the voice of the Lord saying to me, "You were rejected, but not dejected." I answered the Holy Spirit and said, "Aren't they one and the same?" I researched the words, and to my amazement, the Holy Spirit was on point. They are not the same. The Lord wanted me to know that I survived. Therefore, according to the dictionary, dejected is sad, depressed, dispirited, or without hope. Last time I checked, because you and I are born again, we have hope, hope that makes us not ashamed. The psalmist said in Psalm 3, "For thou oh Lord are a shield for me, the glory and the lifter of my head." Therefore, despair is not a part of our package. I sent it right back where it belonged— to the devil.

We will never claim these three Ds as long as we live: depression, dispirited, and despair. No, oh no, we will decree and declare that we are more than conqueror. We will *delight* ourselves in the Lord. He will *deliver* us, and we can *depend* upon him. It was confirmed in my spirit that God prevented me from falling into utter despair. He wanted me to know that yes the first part is true; I was rejected. But because of his tender love and mercy, he didn't let me fall into utter darkness. I needed to live and be in good spirits because I have three lives that needed me to survive. I have lives to touch. I made it and continue to make it because my testimony will help others to stand.

It was not long after that I got the title for the book. As plain as the day, the spirit of the Lord said, "The title of the book is *Rejected but Not Dejected*." I wrote it down, but a few weeks later, I ripped up the paper, but it was still written in my spirit. In April 2016, I was in a Sunday worship service, and the man of God started to minister to me. He said a few things, and then he said, "I see the book." I smiled because I didn't know him, and he didn't know me, but the Holy Spirit knows us both. In January of 2017, another man of God was speaking in the service where I was in attendance. He said, "Many of you here right now God has given you books to write, so write them." I didn't need any more sign, God has spoken now more than once and here I am today obeying him.

I just want to encourage my sisters and brothers who have travelled the road of rejection. Don't allow the enemy to bring you down. You have to know the God that you serve and have a personal relationship with. Give him everything. Cry to him when you have to, ask him to help and deliver you, he will. It is amazing the strength that comes from God. It refreshes your soul. I never sought a Christian therapist or any therapist. I couldn't pay for one. I relied totally on the Holy Spirit to be my comforter, counselor, and my guide.

He carried me safely through. I don't even know sometimes how I made it, but I did. I pray that if there are no children involved after the split, take time to heal yourself. If there are child or children involved, please put their best interest first. Don't use them as pawns between the both of you. Don't let the pain speak for you, and you end up applying more pain to the wound. Take responsibility for your actions and your behavior. They are God's precious gift. Do whatever is possible to kill the spirit of anger and hatred. Let love and forgiveness be the antidote to every negative feelings so that the wounds will heal as quickly as possible.

After you have survived, reach back and pull a sister or a brother out and through. Prayer is the proven weapon. God hears us out of heaven, and he heals our land. I know the other big bad spirit that we have to conquer is fear. It is the pain of the past that can hinder the joys of the future. After you have been healed, and God wants to give you a helpmate, don't run away and hide. I wanted to have what I saw lived before me. My parents have been together for forty-eight years, so of course, when I got married, I was in it for the long haul. I am opening up to the possibilities that I could find love again. The next time, God is going to give me a good godly man. He is going to remember my past pain and gives me double for all my troubles. I wrote this book not for fame, but because I don't do anything unless the Lord bids me to. I hate do overs. So I try to live and get it right as quickly as I can.

I advise you to spend a lot of time in praise and worship. Also, have an active prayer life. Stay close to good friends and family for support, but whatever you do, don't fall into despair. As you send up your praise, worship, and prayer it becomes a memorial before the father, and you can always make a withdrawal whenever you need help. You have to know that the stone that the builders rejected will become the chief cornerstone. I heard an encouragement by Bishop

Jakes, he said, "When people walk out of your life, let them go." I encourage you to let them go. Let go and truly let God. I know that it will be good again.

You see, we need God, and without him, we will be a complete mess. You and I have to let go of all our emotions and serve God because of who we know him to be. He is a restorer, provider, healer, our *I Am that I Am*. Sometimes like Job, we have been asked about and bragged about, and we have no clue to this. You see, God bragged about Job, and Satan asked for him; but one thing you should remember, God gave Satan a limit. We know that the enemy walks around looking for someone to devour, but the life giver is inside of you and I. We shall have life and life more abundantly. For whatever test, we have a testimony. It is after we go through the test, that the oil of God is poured out on us.

So when you don't know what to do, open the Bible and pull a page out of the many witnesses that has gone before us. After Job lost everything, the Bible said, He bowed himself to the ground and worshipped God. "And said, Naked came I out of my mother's womb and naked shall I return thither: the Lord gave, and the Lord hath taken away, blessed be the name of the Lord." You see, though he was slayed, yet he trusted God. The story didn't end until God turned the captivity of Job after he prayed for his friends, and he was blessed with twice as much as he had before. You and I didn't go through just because it is a fixed course, and in the end, we shall come forth as pure gold. I was told that God gives the fiercest battle to his strongest warrior... give God the Glory. You are so strong! You are a warrior, and you will win!

He is a God that is immutable. He cannot lie. He will do just as he says. You have to know that God won't take from you and not bless you in return. He loves you and I.

He is passionate about us, and he wants us to know that he will and can do for us what no other power can do. It is in these tough times we get to see what we are made of. We must pay close attention and learn from our mistakes. Our eyes will be wide open to see what we could have done differently. For example, if I had it to do all over again, I would have dated him more. It is not enough to speak on the phone. There are somethings that we can only learn by being around the person. Also, we will always get a fresh revelation of who God is. It is one thing to read or hear others' testimony. But glory be to God when you have your own. Throughout this ordeal, I can say I know him as Jehovah Shamar, The Lord who keeps, watches, and preserves. I didn't find this in a book. I live this, and I asked Google to give me the Hebrew word for keep. I have proven him to be the *Lord, my keeper.*

Let us pray:

Father, I come before you in the name of Jesus Christ. I humble myself under your mighty hand. Lord, here I am standing before you broken, hurt and rejected. I asked you dear Lord to please wash away the pain. I find myself somewhere I've never been before, and I need your strength to carry me from day to day. Not sure of the path that I should take, but one thing I know for sure is that you promised never to leave me or forsake me. I look to you now for your complete help. I have been rejected, and it hurts really bad, but earth has no sorrow that heaven cannot heal. I need your healing rain to fall down on me. Wash me. Cleanse me, forgive me, and save me from dejection. I need you now… please, oh, God, hear me from your holy heaven, look down, and have mercy on me. I ask dear Lord, today, please remove anger, unforgiveness, and bitterness, I pray. Help me to be like you, father, to forgive the ones who has caused me pain. I need you to hear me, so I'm asking you to help me keep the way clear.

I commit everything into your loving arms, and I know that you will guide me all the way through. In the darkness of my midnight, shine your light right on through. Make yourself be made known unto me your servant. In my own strength, I can do but so much, but with you, I am more than a conqueror. Help me dear Lord, to know that you are my strength, hope, and shield. When my head bowed low, thou, oh Lord, are a shield for me, the glory, and the lifter of my head. I thank you, in advance for renewed joy, vitality, hope. I put my trust in you. You know the path that I take, and after you have tried me, I shall come forth as pure gold. Nothing that happens in my life is without a cause or a purpose because you are the author and the finisher of my faith. I shall, will, and must finish well. I thank you for all that you have done and about to do in me, through me, and by me. I know, dear Lord, that victory is on before, and I will not quit because you don't use quitters. You are a God who take the broken pieces and put them back together again. You oh, Lord, will make something beautiful out of the ashes of my life. I am on humbling myself under your mighty hand, and I know that you will carry me out of this season into a season of joy unspeakable and full of your glory. In the precious name of your son Jesus, we pray and say amen and amen.

Those who have been rejected by the ones they love. Be encouraged! There is hope and your future is bright. I am beaming with great joy on the inside because truly, God sent his words and healed me. You, too, can be healed; just take God at his words.

LIST OF REFERENCE SCRIPTURES QUOTED AND OR PARAPHRASED

Judges 20
Psalm 3:3, Psalm 42:6, Psalm 46:1, and Psalm 90:1 and Psalm 139:8
Job 3:25, Job13:5 and Job 42:10
Isaiah 65:24
Matthew 6:12, 13 and Matthew 26:39
Romans 12:21 and Romans 3:4
Luke 18:1
1 Thessalonians 5:17

ENDNOTES

The Holy Bible
Brainyquotes.com
Dictonary.com
Google.com
Hymnary.org (God Leads Us Along) In shady green pastures so rich
    and so sweet.
Movie: diary of A Mad Black Woman by Tyler Perry

ABOUT THE AUTHOR

Nadine Blackwood-Barnes is an ordained minister in the New Testament Church of God. The church of God has its headquarters in Cleveland, TN. Minister Barnes has served in various ministries in the church: She served as Sunday school secretary, praise and worship, associate pastor and two years as women ministry president. She has a Bachelor's of Arts degree in Sociology, from Hunter College, New York. She is a mother of twin boys, Jayden and Javon Barnes, and daughter Jazmine Barnes. She is passionate about helping the people of God in reaching their destiny despite the painful process. Her truthful, simplistic and sincere way of conveying God's Word under the anointing has appealed to those who come in contact with her.

CPSIA information can be obtained
at www.ICGtesting.com
Printed in the USA
LVHW091836010719
622841LV00001BA/171/P